TABLE OF CONTENTS

INTRODUCTION 01

SESSIONS

Session One: Forming A Leadership Community 07

Session Two: The Masculine Leadership Journey 19

Session Three: Trusting God With Our Fear 29

Session Four: Trusting God With Our Future 39

Session Five: Growing Our Influence 51

Session Six: The Wisdom Of Descent 61

Session Seven: Building Relationships Of Trust 71

Session Eight: Crossing The Threshold Of Our Growth 81

CONCLUSION 92

Copyright © 2019 by Sage Expansion.

All rights reserved. This book or any portion thereof may not be reproduced or used in any manner whatsoever without the express written permission of the publisher except for the use of brief quotations in a book review.

Scripture quotations are from the Holy Bible, New International Version®, NIV® Copyright ©1973, 1978, 1984, 2011 by Biblica, Inc.® Used by permission. All rights reserved worldwide.

Printed in the United States of America

ISBN: 978-0-9985791-1-5

www.SageExpansion.com

A LETTER FROM JACK

Thank you for your willingness to grow as a man and leader.

You have joined a strong community of men who will support your growth and challenge you to deepen your soul, integrate your heart, and expand your influence as a mature spiritual leader.

Nothing could be more important for your family, your profession and our culture than for you to develop your spiritual leadership. This experiential leadership curriculum will help you to become the integrated man and leader that you aspire to be and is so desperately needed in every sector of our society.

A significant challenge for men in leadership today is that most of the opportunities for truly meaningful relationships with one another have been removed from our culture. As men, we have been taught to compete, hide our true feelings and to live in isolation. By participating in this Leader Cohort, you will have an opportunity to support, encourage and strengthen one another in a circle of trust as we engage in the real challenges of life.

Please take advantage of this unique curriculum to engage in a transformative journey of spiritual leadership and to help create a culture where you can bring the power of being an integrated man and leader to your personal, family and professional context.

Jack

Jack Gregory Nicholson

INTRODUCTION

> "The Lord does not look at the things man looks at. Man looks at the outward appearance, but the Lord looks at the heart."
>
> 1 Samuel 16:7b

BIBLICAL FOUNDATION: THE LIFE AND LEADERSHIP OF KING DAVID

This leader development experience is designed to develop and strengthen your character, capacity and competency for spiritual leadership with a trusted group of committed peers. Each session, we will look at King David's journey toward authentic spiritual leadership, and together we will ask how God is at work in similar ways in our own lives.

The curriculum itself combines the best processes of spiritual formation, leader development and experiential learning to help emerging and established leaders fulfill their God-given calling and destiny. Be assured that the teachings, group processes and experiential learning in this manual have been field tested and proven to powerfully impact both ministry and marketplace leaders like you.

King David was a remarkable spiritual leader whose deep and powerful influence continues to resonate with many people today. Here is what God himself thought of the heart of David:

"The Spirit of the Lord came upon David in Power." (I Samuel 16:13)

"I have found David son of Jesse a man after my own heart; he will do everything I want him to do." (Acts 13:22b)

LEADER DEVELOPMENT CURRICULUM

01 The Leadership Roundtable

The Leadership Roundtable is an important part of the development process that involves a 3-hour monthly training event, experiential learning, accountability and support for each person within a circle of trust. Being engaged in this leadership community where men can grow and learn together is perhaps the most critical component of the *Spiritual Leadership* Curriculum. Your commitment and engagement at every meeting, unless there is an emergency or personal crisis, is essential to the process.

02 Vision & Purpose of Leader Development

The purpose of the leader development curriculum is to develop high-capacity spiritual leaders who will guide and mentor their relationships of trust to advance the Kingdom of God in the world. Each member of the Leader Cohort will seek to create a culture of whole-hearted leadership where grace, wisdom and love are practiced in his personal and professional context.

03 Values of the Leadership Community

Knowing and embracing the essential values of the Leadership Community will help you and your Cohort to grow in spiritual maturity and function as a group in a healthy and vibrant way. Frederick Buechner has beautifully expressed these core values in the following statement:

> *"The place God calls you to is the place where your deep gladness and the world's deep hunger meet."* [1]

In this quote, Buechner makes several assumptions that are vital to our gathering as leaders and to the convictions that the Leadership Community holds dear:

GOD IS REALLY THERE AND HE IS PERSONAL.

He is not the subjective new age god who some say can be found within all of us. He is not the pantheistic god who is seen in all of nature. Nor is he the impersonal force that is out there somewhere directing the universe. This is the God of the Hebrew and Christian Scriptures who is personal, loving and holy; who knows our names and is deeply involved with our lives in the unfolding of redemptive history.

GOD IS CALLING YOU TO BE A MAN OF SIGNIFICANT INFLUENCE.

Abraham was called out of his homeland of Ur. Joseph was called to provide resources to his starving family. Moses was called to lead the Israelites out of captivity. Jeremiah was called to intercede for his nation in rapid decline. God is calling every man to advance his Kingdom in the world—right where you are, right now.

---

[1] Buechner, F. (1993). *Wishful Thinking: A Seeker's ABC.* New York: HarperCollins. pp. 118–119.

YOU ARE THE STEWARD OF A DEEP GLADNESS, A GOD-GIVEN DESIGN.

You are a very unique leader with a particular set of abilities, talents and gifts. This deep design must be understood and aligned with your sense of personal calling, stewardship and destiny. Your life story with all the joy, pain, brokenness and failures is like a beautiful work of art, needing to be embraced, embodied and fully expressed in a meaningful way.

OUR WORLD IS STARVING FOR SPIRITUAL LEADERSHIP.

Many in our culture are longing for a stronger sense of meaning and purpose in their lives. Without a connection to churches, neighborhoods or extended families, people experience a profound sense of alienation and loss of community. Mature spiritual leadership stands in this cultural and spiritual gap and provides hope for a postmodern world that is desperately searching for meaning and community today.

WE ARE CREATED FOR THE CONVERGENCE OF DESIGN, DESIRE AND DESTINY.

God wants you to experience the joining of your strengths, talents and capacities in a life context that fulfills the desires of your heart (Ps. 37:4-6). This convergence is sometimes described as the "sweet spot" or the exhilarating experience of being "in the flow." We believe that every leader is capable of aligning his life with this joyful intersection of gifting, purpose and service.

The Leadership Roundtable is an authentic experience of community structured to help you find this convergence where calling and need, design and destiny meet. It is at this point of convergence that we believe you can be a powerful influence for God in all of your life relationships. The Leader Cohort you are joining is carefully designed to help you take stock of your life, recognize the wonders and shadows in your soul, and to energize your God-given calling as you become a man and leader of destiny.

04 Leadership Challenges

Each Leadership Roundtable will have a theme and the focus of the experiential work will be on your current leadership challenges. A leadership challenge can arise from your family responsibilities, professional aspirations or missional endeavors. What is important is to bring to each Roundtable meeting an awareness of where you are focusing your energy, and that usually involves a current leadership challenge that you are facing in the present moment.

05 The Edge of Your Growth

The personal transformational journey requires that you consciously stay at the edge of your growth. This is difficult to do, as we can be preoccupied with the past or anxious and concerned about our future. Yet it is at the edge of our growth that we experience our true selves in relationship with the holy, healing and loving presence of God. The best way to become a transformational leader is to integrate the light and dark sides of our soul in the presence of God right at the edge of our growth. This is the work of each leader with the support and accountability of other men in relationships of trust.

06 Covenant of the Leadership Community

The Leadership Roundtable is an opportunity for you to be in community with other ministry and marketplace leaders who are on a transformative spiritual journey. Authenticity, transparency and genuineness are the result of being in loving relationships of trust. To build a circle of trust in an environment of grace, it is important to create a sacred space where it is safe to look at our lives and share from our hearts.

The Roundtable Covenant is a helpful tool that guides and protects us as we meet to explore our souls and share the light and dark sides of our leadership. We want you to be familiar with the idea of a covenant and understand how it can serve as a unifying and bonding experience for each Roundtable gathering.

Authenticity	I will be who I am without masks and facades.
Honesty	I will look inside myself and say what I truly feel.
Integrity	I will do what I say I will do.
Reliability	I will be present and available at all the meetings.
Spirituality	I will open my heart to God.
Confidentiality	I will keep everything in confidence that is said in this group.
Intentionality	I will do what God reveals to me and leads me to do.
Availability	I will be there for another man who asks for my support.
Accountability	I will give the members of this Cohort permission to confront me if I am out of integrity with what I say and do.

_____ _____
Signature   Date

> "Take delight in the Lord, and he will give you the desires of your heart. Commit your way to the Lord; trust in him and he will do this: He will make your righteous reward shine like the dawn, your vindication like the noonday sun.
>
> Psalm 37:4–6

FORMING A LEADERSHIP COMMUNITY

01

Session One

01

FORMING A LEADERSHIP COMMUNITY
Session One

 ## INTRODUCE THEME

Learning a foreign language requires mastering the fundamentals of vocabulary, syntax and grammar. This is also true with the language and structure of holistic leader development. In Session One: Forming a Leadership Community, we will review the vision and purpose of the *Spiritual Leadership* Curriculum, introduce key concepts for integrated leadership, and outline the structure and process for building a powerful leadership community.

 ## LEARNING OBJECTIVES

- Participants will grasp the vision and purpose of Spiritual Leadership.

- Participants will understand the conceptual framework that supports their growth and development as a man and leader.

- Participants will understand and engage the major components of the leader development process in order to build trust and bond with their peers.

- Participants will commit to experiential learning in order to grow and develop their capacity as spiritual leaders.

- Participants will take the risk of personal transparency and vulnerability to become a transformational leadership community.

 ## LEARNING PLAN

- Inclusion & centering
- Learning & dialogue
- Personal reflection
- Roundtable meal & group process
- Experiential exercise
- Second exercise or break-out groups
- Takeaways & closing ritual

LEARNING OUTLINE (40-45 min.)

- **Men in our culture are longing for greater meaning and community in their lives.**
- **Vision and Purpose of Leader Development:**
  - Develop high capacity spiritual leaders who will influence and mentor their relationships of trust to advance the Kingdom of God in the world.
  - Create a culture of integrated leadership where grace, wisdom, and love are practiced in each man's personal and professional context.
- **Scriptural Foundation for the Leader Development Process:**
  - The Life and Leadership of King David (1 Samuel 16—2 Samuel 24)
  - Spiritual Leadership as an expression of the Great Commandment (Mark 12:30)
  - Embodying as disciples the glory, grace and truth of Jesus Christ (John 1:14)
- **Key Components of the Leader Development Curriculum** — Exhibit 1
- **The Human Architecture of Transformative Leadership Community** — Exhibit 2
  - Design to Destiny
  - Human Systems Polarity
  - Quadrant Leadership
  - Circle of Trust
- **The Great Commandment in Four Dimensions of Reality** — Exhibit 3
- **The Transformational Leadership Pathway** — Exhibit 4
  - Learn
  - Experience
  - Integrate
  - Execute

PERSONAL REFLECTION (5-10 min.)

EXPERIENTIAL EXERCISE (30-45 min.)
Exercise One: Exploring the Ideal & Shadow Side of your Leadership.

NOTES

EXHIBIT 1   *Forming a Leadership Community*

LEADER DEVELOPMENT COMPONENTS

BONDING EXPERIENCE — Gathering together as a new leader cohort, getting to know each other, sharing our stories and building a circle of trust.

LEADERSHIP ROUNDTABLE — Monthly leadership training, experiential learning, accountability and support for each person within a committed leadership community.

MENTORING & COACHING — Receiving wise counsel, guidance and spiritual direction for personal, leadership and organizational challenges.

DEVELOPMENT PLAN — Synthesizing individual and group feedback that results in measurable goals and practical outcomes for personal and professional development.

PEER SUPPORT — Engaging two or three peers for personal support, interactive learning, mutual accountability and addressing each other's leadership challenges.

TRANSFORMATIVE RETREAT — A powerful experience of authentic community and transformative learning that releases the unique identity, character and courage of the leader.

INTEGRATION PROJECT — Implementing a real-time project that integrates leader growth and development with guidance and support from mentors.

CELEBRATION EVENT — A final gathering as a community of men where we share and celebrate how we have grown from our experience in leader development.

EXHIBIT 2

Forming a Leadership Community

Your leadership is only as valuable as the **people** and **teams** who follow your efforts. Without the efforts of talented people who are willing to work together to achieve common vision, purpose and goals, there is really no impact or social value. Nothing is more important for a spiritual leader than to design and resource the human architecture of a powerful leadership community.

FOUR CRITICAL DIMENSIONS OF LEADERSHIP COMMUNITY

① Design to Destiny

- Metaphor: The Arrow
- Alignment of leadership roles around each person's unique abilities.
- Freedom comes from recognizing and letting go of those activities that don't engage your vision, purpose and passion.
- How can I express my unique ability more fully in my leadership?

② Human Systems Polarity

- Metaphor: The Infinity Loop
- Growth of the leader and the organization are inseparable.
- Leaders have the responsibility of keeping their enterprises in PRIME.
- How do I maintain balance between individual and organizational growth?

③ Quadrant Leadership

- Metaphor: The Quadrants
- Building the human architecture requires sound blueprints.
- Mind, heart, soul & strength are required for transformative leadership.
- How can I be more integrated and whole-hearted in my leadership?

④ Circles of Trust

- Metaphor: The Circle
- Effective organizations are built upon relationships of trust.
- A leadership community has high emotional intelligence, capacity for crucial conversations and transforms conflict into constructive energy.
- How can we build relationships of trust in our leadership community?

EXHIBIT 3 *Forming a Leadership Community*

FOUR DIMENSIONS OF REALITY

We all have a unique view of the world where our perspective on reality can be very different from others. Seeing realities and worldviews from four distinct quadrants gives us the ability to be more effective in leading constructive change and transforming conflict into purposeful energy. What dominant worldview is your reality most like, and where does your energy flow from one quadrant to another?

MIND — Unitary Worldview	STRENGTH — Sensory Worldview
Policies	Actions
Rules	Behaviors
Theories	Facts
Truths	Data
Creeds	Objects
Principles	Material Things
Designs	Resources
Belief Systems	Events
Structures	Experiences
Assumptions	Sensuality
WHAT WILL WE DO?	**HOW SHALL WE DO IT?**
SOUL — Mythical Worldview	**HEART** — Social Worldview
Vision	Values
Symbols	Feelings
Meanings	Preferences
Opportunities	What Matters
Metaphors	Purposes
Stories	Wants
Dreams	Motivations
Inventions	Relationships
Inspirations	Attitudes
Creations	Appreciation
WHY SHOULD WE DO IT?	**WHO WILL DO IT?**

Adapted from McWhinney, W., Webber, J. B., Smith, D. M., & Novokowsky, B. J. (1997). Creating paths of change: Managing issues and resolving problems in organizations. Sage.

EXHIBIT 4

Forming a Leadership Community

TRANSFORMATIONAL LEADERSHIP PATHWAY

Whenever spiritual leaders are facilitating deep change, it is important to go below the line of just learning and execution. Facilitators must help a person to experience and then integrate their life challenges at the heart level. Then one's shadow and resistance can be integrated into the soul before being put into action. Holistic change will naturally lead to congruent and spirit empowered behavior.

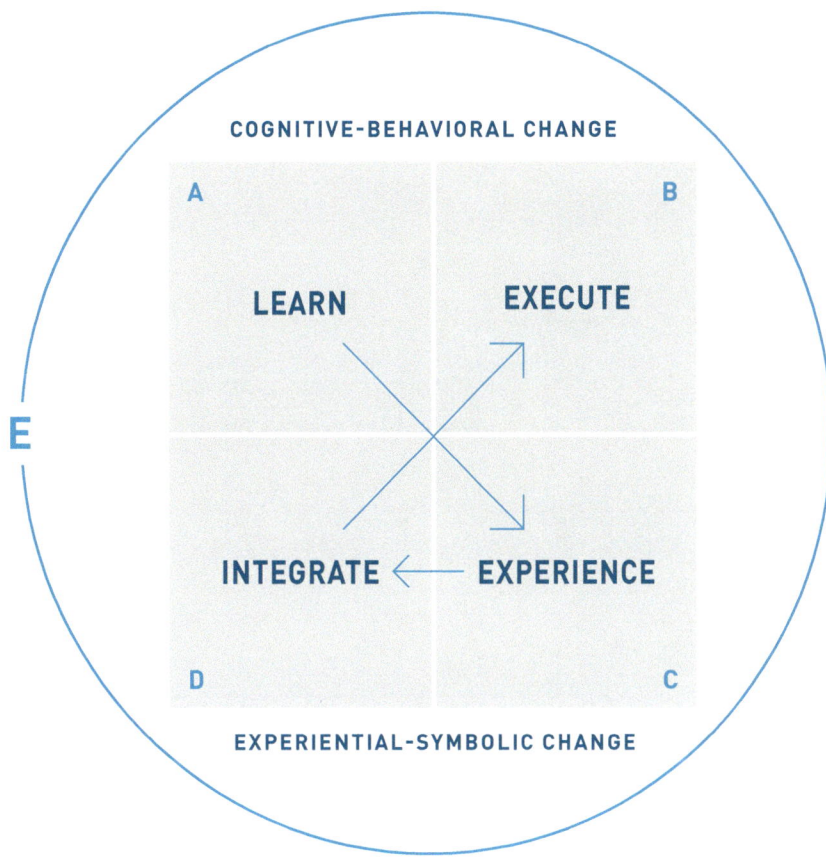

LEVELS OF INFLUENCE

A	Transferring knowledge	(Teaching)
B	Developing skills	(Training)
C	Shifting values	(Coaching)
D	Building character	(Mentoring)
E	Embodying leadership	(Circle of Trust)

The catalyst for change is transformative interpersonal relationships.

PERSONAL REFLECTION
Forming a Leadership Community

(Share During Meal or Break-Out Groups | 5-7 mins.)

1. What is your dominant reality or worldview?

2. What factors shaped and influenced your dominant reality or worldview?

3. Which Quadrant is the source of your leadership energy? Give examples.

4. To what Quadrant does your leadership energy tend to flow? Why is this so?

5. Are you primarily an "Upper Quadrant" or "Lower Quadrant" leader? Explain.

NOTES

INTEGRATION & APPLICATION
Forming a Leadership Community

Nothing is more important for a spiritual leader than to design and resource the human architecture of a powerful leadership community.

How do you envision becoming a more influential man and spiritual leader?
What do you anticipate being your greatest leadership challenge?

. . . .

Which of the Leader Development Components do you look forward to?
Which component are you most anxious about or resistant to?

. . . .

Read, reflect and journal through the life of David (1 Samuel 16—2 Samuel 24).

. . . .

Write down what you need from your mentor and peers to become an integrated man and leader.
Share what you need in your one-to-one meetings with your mentor and peers.

. . . .

As a member of the Leadership Roundtable, what do you plan to contribute
toward the formation of a powerful leadership community?

NOTES

02

THE MASCULINE LEADERSHIP JOURNEY

Session Two

02

THE MASCULINE LEADERSHIP JOURNEY
Session Two

 INTRODUCE THEME

The mature man is essential for gracious, wise and loving spiritual leadership. You cannot have one without the other. In a culture that denigrates traditional masculine roles, a man must trust his essential nature and the purpose that God has placed in his heart. In Session Two: The Masculine Leadership Journey, we will explore the Life and Leadership of King David, who was known as a man after God's own heart. He developed his deep and passionate character over a lifetime of trusting God throughout his leadership journey.

 LEARNING OBJECTIVES

- Participants will appreciate the leadership journey of King David, who was described by God as a man after his own heart.

- Participants will comprehend how masculine development normally progresses through the adult lifespan.

- Participants will internalize the meaning and power of the Four Masculine Archetypes: KING—WARRIOR—LOVER—SAGE.

- Participants will utilize the Four Masculine Archetypes to evaluate their own character development as a man and leader.

- Participants will trust the wisdom and strength of their masculine soul to engage their current leadership challenges.

 LEARNING PLAN

- Inclusion & centering
- Learning & dialogue
- Personal reflection
- Roundtable meal & group process
- Experiential exercise
- Second exercise or break-out groups
- Takeaways & closing ritual

LEARNING OUTLINE (40-45 min.)

- **Men need a transcendent purpose to be fulfilled (Churchill in WWII)**
- **The long spiritual preparation of a man and leader:**
  - Becoming a spiritual leader requires unusual depth and commitment
  - The personal transformation of King David took a lifetime to complete
  - Your character is more important to God than your accomplishments
- **The Life and Leadership of King David** — Exhibit 1
  - A man after God's own heart (Acts 13:22)
  - David the Mighty Warrior (Incredible Military Victories)
  - David the Magnificent King (Unified the Nation of Israel)
  - David the Seasoned Sage (Wrote most of the Psalms)
- **Introduction to the Masculine Archetypes** — Exhibit 2
  - King: Capacity for Blessing
  - Warrior: Capacity for Service
  - Lover: Capacity for Relationship
  - Sage: Capacity for Wisdom
- **Understanding the Gold & Shadow side of the Masculine Soul**
- **The Normal Progression of Masculine Development:**
  - Attached as a Child (solid core)
  - Established as an Adult (20-30's)
  - Empowered as a Leader (40-50's)
  - Matured as a Man (60-70's)
- **God exalted David and his Kingdom for the sake of his people (2 Samuel 5:9-12)**
- **God's incredible promise and David's heartfelt response (2 Samuel 7:8f)**

> "I will praise the Lord who counsels me; even at night my heart instructs me. I have set the Lord always before me. Because he is at my right hand, I will not be shaken."
>
> Psalm 16:7–8

PERSONAL REFLECTION (5-10 min.)

EXPERIENTIAL EXERCISE (30-45 min.)
Exercise Two: Drawing Wisdom & Strength from the Masculine Soul

NOTES
_____
_____
_____
_____

EXHIBIT 1 *The Masculine Leadership Journey*

LIFE AND LEADERSHIP OF KING DAVID
I SAMUEL 16 — 2 SAMUEL 24

KING
(40s — 50s)

+ David anointed as King
+ Absalom the Dark Prince
+ David abdicates his Power

OWNING OUR POWER

WARRIOR
(20s — 30s)

+ David kills Goliath
+ David's military victories
+ David's restraint with Saul

TRUSTING OUR MISSION

SAGE
(60s — 70s)

+ The Wisdom of Descent
+ Shadow work in the Psalms
+ David seasoned by Life

GROWING OUR CHARACTER

LOVER
(Lifespan)

+ David's friendship with Jonathan
+ David's adultery with Bathsheba
+ David's passionate love for God

ENGAGING OUR HEART

DAVID AND THE MASCULINE LEADERSHIP JOURNEY

EXHIBIT 2 The Masculine Leadership Journey

THE MASCULINE ARCHETYPES

KING
Capacity for Blessing

GOLD	SHADOW
Order	Tyrant
Blessing	Paranoid
Integrity	Defensive
Steward	Greedy
Balance	Exploitive
Authority	Controlling
Provider	Intolerant
Generosity	Insecure
Abundance	Shaming
Authentic	Abdicator

WARRIOR
Capacity for Service

GOLD	SHADOW
Discipline	Oppositional
Focus	Fundamentalist
Loyalty	Cruel
Mission	Demeaning
Assertion	Distant
Service	Abrasive
Sacrifice	Compulsive
Risk	Abusive
Vigilant	Narrow
Strategist	Sadistic

SAGE
Capacity for Wisdom

GOLD	SHADOW
Insightful	Trickster
Healer	Seducer
Awareness	Untruthful
Trustworthy	Manipulator
Discernment	Elitist
Reflective	Con Artist
Prayerful	Charlatan
Mentor	Scarcity
Elder	Prideful
Guide	Guru

LOVER
Capacity for Relationship

GOLD	SHADOW
Intimacy	Dependent
Nurture	Addicted
Artistic	Playboy
Expressive	Non-assertive
Connected	Self-serving
Passionate	Egocentric
Spiritual	Spineless
Giving	Unsatisfied
Faithful	Narcissistic
Sexual	Restless

PERSONAL REFLECTION
The Masculine Leadership Journey

(Share During Meal or Break-Out Groups | 5-7 mins.)

1. Which archetype best describes your masculine character?

2. Make a list of the gold and shadow sides of your character.

3. What would you like to change about your character?

4. Describe the current life-stage of your masculine journey.

5. What would you like to emulate in the life and leadership of David?

NOTES

INTEGRATION & APPLICATION

The Masculine Leadership Journey

Your character is more important to God than your accomplishments.

Identify in the life of David the major turning points in the development of his character.

· · · ·

Develop a timeline that identifies the turning points and defining moments that have shaped your life and character.

· · · ·

Share the meaning and significance of your timeline in your one-to-one meeting with your mentor and peers. What feedback did you receive from your mentor and peers?

· · · ·

How do you intend to integrate the Gold and Shadow sides of your leadership? What part of your Shadow are you most likely to hide or find resistant to change?

· · · ·

Pray with faith and openness about undertaking the long spiritual preparation that is necessary for you to become a wise, loving and gracious leader.

NOTES

03

TRUSTING GOD WITH OUR FEAR

Session Three

03

TRUSTING GOD WITH OUR FEAR
Session Three

 ## INTRODUCE THEME

Sometimes it is difficult to trust God with our fear. Leaders are not always aware of the depth of their fears and don't know how to process them with God in faith. When they face terrifying threats in their lives, they cope with their fear with various degrees of denial and bravado. In Session Three, we can learn how to explore our fears and access the faith and courage we need to confront our Goliath. We can be like David who relied upon his story, his strengths and his God to defeat the Giant that threatened everything that was precious to him.

 ## LEARNING OBJECTIVES

- Participants will allow themselves to identify and accept their fears.
- Participants will learn how to hold the tension between faith and fear.
- Participants will learn how David relied upon his faith and found the courage to confront and defeat Goliath.
- Participants will identify the greatest threat or "Giant" in their lives.
- Participants will explore the depth of their faith and fear as they find the courage to overcome their Giant.

 ## LEARNING PLAN

- Inclusion & centering
- Learning & dialogue
- Personal Reflection
- Roundtable meal & group process
- Experiential exercise
- Second exercise or break-out groups
- Takeaways & closing ritual

LEARNING OUTLINE (40-45 min.)

- George Washington's intense fear during the Revolutionary War [1]
- Great leaders can hold the tension of faith and fear:
  - Relationship between fear and declining performance
  - Acceptance, assimilation and integration of fear
  - Deeper fear—the fear of being found out
  - How have you struggled with fear?
- Overwhelming fear helps us to rely upon God and not on ourselves (2 Corinthians 1:8-11).
- David was chosen and strengthened by God to fulfill his mission:
  - He was an initiated man of power (1 Samuel 16:13)
  - He knew that God was with him (1 Samuel 17:45-46)
  - He could trust God with his fear (Psalm 27:1-3)
- David faced an overwhelming leadership challenge - Exhibit 1
- David had the courage to confront and kill Goliath (1 Samuel 17)
  - Saul was immobilized by fear
  - David was emboldened by faith
  - What are you willing to fight for?
- David's faith, preparation, and courage enabled him to overcome his fear:
  - He told his Story (killed the lion & the bear - 1 Samuel 17:34-37)
  - He knew his Strengths (took his sling, not Saul's armor - 1 Samuel 17:38-40)
  - He trusted his God (for the battle is the Lord's - 1 Samuel 17:47)
- Would God call us to an impossible mission that we could not fulfill?

PERSONAL REFLECTION (5-10 min.)

EXPERIENTIAL EXERCISE (30-45 min.)
Exercise Three: Exploring the Depth of our Faith and Fear

NOTES

---

[1] McCullough, D. (2006) 1776. New York; Simon & Schuster.

DAVID'S OVERWHELMING LEADERSHIP CHALLENGE

Every leader has faced, or will face, his unique battle with "Goliath." He will experience some major challenge in the private or professional arena of his life that seems overwhelming and well beyond his resources. The story of David killing Goliath provides a wealth of encouragement for all of us as we engage our threatening leadership challenges. The story also presents each of us with the very real choice of whether we confront our "Goliath" with faith or fear.

Fear is Natural

It is important to understand that our fear is natural and nothing to be ashamed of. Fear is a common emotion we all experience, even for the most successful leaders. The objective is not to become fearless or anxiety free, but to learn how to respond to our leadership challenges courageously and effectively.

David and Goliath

The story of David and Goliath is an ancient one, yet remarkably relevant for every leader facing an intimidating set of circumstances. This familiar Hebrew story informs us that every overwhelming leadership challenge involves these common, fear-producing elements:

Poor Odds

Goliath was over nine feet tall and David was a teenage boy. On the basis of size alone, David was no match for his opponent. At times we are scared for a very good reason. The odds may be stacked against us and from a human point of view the outcome doesn't look very promising.

Profound Isolation

Goliath taunted the entire Israelite army by asking them to "Give me a man" to fight him to the death. His challenge required that one man would have to step out of the ranks and face this giant alone. All eyes would be on that man and he would carry an enormous weight of responsibility. If David lost, all would be lost.

Persistent Opposition

The Bible says that "for forty days the Philistine took his stand every morning and evening" and successfully intimidated Saul and the Israeli Army. Goliath used the effective tactic of wearing down his opposition. Some of our challengers are very persistent and will try to wear down our resistance through fear and doubt.

Inadequate Resources

Goliath ridiculed David by saying "Am I a dog that you came at me with sticks?" David had reason to fear a man with one hundred and twenty-five pounds of armor and a spear with a fifteen-pound head. In contrast, David had a sling with five smooth stones. How often have we felt inadequate and unprepared for the enormous challenge that we are facing and listened to the voice of doubt?

Intense Shame

David's oldest brother attacked him with sarcastic accusations: "I know your presumption and the evil in your heart, for you have come down to see the battle!" King Saul reminds David that he is only a boy and the Philistine was a man of war. These were the critical voices that said "You are not enough" for the task at hand. David had to overcome the psychological barrier of shame by trusting that God would not fail the mission he had given him.

Enormous Risk

Goliath threatened the Israelites by saying, "You will become our subjects and serve us" and "I will give your flesh to the beasts of the field." Leaders face financial, relational, and professional risks that are very real and their decisions are often accompanied by far-reaching consequences. David trusted how the hand of the Lord had been upon him. He knew that God would deliver him.

"The Lord is my light and my salvation – whom shall I fear?

The Lord is the stronghold of my life –

Of whom shall I be afraid?"

Psalm 27:1

"It is not by sword or spear that the Lord saves; for the battle is the Lord's..."

1 Samuel 17:47

PERSONAL REFLECTION
Trusting God With Our Fear

[Share During Meal or Break-Out Groups (5-7 mins.)]

1. Describe the Giant that you are confronting in your life?

2. Write down what you are afraid of at this time.

3. What would happen if you gave in to fear?

4. What would happen if you responded in faith?

5. If you had the courage, what would you do about the Giant in your life?

NOTES

INTEGRATION & APPLICATION
Trusting God With Our Fear

Overwhelming fear helps us to rely upon God and not ourselves.

Identify the threats and intimidating circumstances you are currently facing in your life and leadership. Take the time to journal about your faith and fear.

· · · ·

Wrestle with the deeper fear of being found out. Be willing to confront areas of your life that are shameful and bring them into the presence of God.

· · · ·

David overcame his fear by knowing his story and trusting God with his strengths. Write down how God has prepared you for a great leadership challenge.

· · · ·

What are the financial, relational and professional risks for you if you don't confront your intimidating giant? Share these risks with your peer group.

· · · ·

There was a lot at stake for David and Israel when Goliath challenged him. In your current leadership context, what are you willing to fight for?

NOTES

04

TRUSTING GOD WITH OUR FUTURE

Session Four

04

TRUSTING GOD WITH OUR FUTURE
Session Four

 ## INTRODUCE THEME

Every leader carries anxiety about the future. Sometimes that anxiety becomes so intense that one becomes obsessive and willful about controlling the future instead of trusting God for his timing and provision. In Session Four, we learn that King Saul became very angry, jealous and violent in response to David's growing power and influence. Instead of trusting God with his future, he turned to force to hold onto his Kingdom. As leaders, we want to rely upon authentic spiritual power and not force to accomplish our vision, mission and purpose.

 ## LEARNING OBJECTIVES

- Participants will allow themselves to identify and accept their fears.
- Participants will understand the difference between Power and Force.
- Participants will learn how David was able to trust God with his future, whereas Saul relied upon force to manage his anxiety and loss of control.
- Participants will become aware of how they need to trust God when they are being tested in the midst of their personal transformational journey.
- Participants will explore whether they will turn to Power or Force in dealing with a serious threat to their future.

 ## LEARNING PLAN

- Inclusion & centering
- Learning & dialogue
- Personal Reflection
- Roundtable meal & group process
- Experiential exercise
- Second exercise or break-out groups
- Takeaways & closing ritual

LEARNING OUTLINE (40–45 min.)

- **Two Kinds of Wrenches: Crescent ("Don't Force It!") or Socket (Applied Power)**
- **Power is qualitatively different than Force** – Exhibit 1
- **There are three different kinds of power that a Spiritual Leader can exercise:**
  - Control Power
  - Influence Power
  - Appreciative Power
- **Appreciative Inquiry is the exploration of what gives life to human systems when they function at their best.** [2] – Exhibit 2
- **God is all powerful and yet doesn't force his will upon us (Philippians 2)**
- **David, in contrast to Saul, entrusted God with his Future (1 Samuel 18-31)**
  - David knew he was annointed as the future King of Israel (1 Samuel 16:13)
  - David relied upon authentic spiritual power, not the force of his will
- **King Saul relied upon force to hold onto his Kingdom:**
  - Conspiring to have David killed (1 Samuel 18)
  - Attempting to assassinate David in his home (1 Samuel 19)
  - Killing the Priests and their families at Nob (1 Samuel 22)
  - Hunting David down in the wilderness (1 Samuel 23-26)
- **David resisted opportunities to take the Kingdom by force:**
  - Killing Saul inside a cave (1 Samuel 24)
  - Slaughtering the household of Nabal (1 Samuel 25)
  - Killing Saul in his sleep (1 Samuel 26)
  - Forming an alliance with the Philistines (1 Samuel 27)
- **In the end, Saul was ultimately destroyed by his willfulness, jealousy, pride and obsessive need for control (1 Samuel 28 & 31)**
- **David was determined to trust God for his provision and timing (1 Samuel 26:8-11)**
- **Trusting God is difficult in the Personal Transformational Journey** – Exhibit 3

PERSONAL REFLECTION (5–10 min.)

EXPERIENTIAL EXERCISE (30–45 min.)
Exercise Four: Exploring the Trajectory of your Future

---

[2] Whitney, D. & Trosten-Bloom, A. (2003). The power of appreciative inquiry: A practical guide to positive change. San Francisco, CA: Berrett-Koehler Publishers, Inc.

EXHIBIT 1

POWER VS. FORCE

"Power is always associated with that which supports the significance of life itself. It appeals to that part of human nature that we call noble—in contrast to force, which appeals to that which we call crass. Power appeals to what uplifts, dignifies and enables. Force must always be justified, whereas power requires no justification. Force is associated with the partial, Power with the whole."

"Force always moves against something, whereas Power doesn't move against anything at all. Force is incomplete and therefore has to be fed energy constantly… Power in contrast, energizes, gives forth, supplies and supports. Power gives life and energy—force takes these away."

DAVID R. HAWKINS (2012), POWER VS. FORCE.

EXHIBIT 2   *Trusting God With Our Future*

APPRECIATIVE POWER

"The power of Appreciative Inquiry occurs when the appreciation and inquiry are combined. Like the elements hydrogen and oxygen that combine to make water—the most nurturing substance on earth—appreciation and inquiry combine to produce a vital and powerful, catalytic effect on leadership and organization change."

**DIANA WHITNEY & AMANDA TROSTEN-BLOOM (2003),
THE POWER OF APPRECIATIVE INQUIRY.**

EXHIBIT 3

PERSONAL TRANSFORMATIONAL JOURNEY

AWARENESS → RESISTANCE → DEEP CHANGE → OVERCOMING

CIRCLES OF TRUST PROVIDE MEANING AND SUPPORT THROUGH THE JOURNEY.

NOTES

PERSONAL REFLECTION
Trusting God With Our Future

[Share During Meal or Break-Out Groups | 5-7 mins.]

WHERE DO YOU LIVE MOST OFTEN?

PAST	PRESENT	FUTURE
GUILT & SHAME	DEEP TRUST	ANXIETY & FEAR

1. What are you most concerned about when you are thinking about your future?

2. What critical decision do you need to make about the direction of your future?

3. If you were to rely upon force, what would you do to determine your future?

4. If you were to draw upon your authentic power, how would you shape your future?

5. If you could fully trust God with your future, what would you do?

© 2019 SAGE EXPANSION | ALL RIGHTS RESERVED.

NOTES

INTEGRATION & APPLICATION
Trusting God With Our Future

As leaders, we want to rely upon authentic spiritual power and not force to accomplish our vision, mission and purpose.

Read 1 Samuel 18-31 and reflect upon the critical times that David trusted God with his future. How would you have responded in those situations?

. . . .

In your leadership at home and in the workplace, how often do you engage in Control Power, Influence Power & Appreciative Power?

. . . .

Describe a time in your life when you responded to a serious threat and loss of control like King Saul? When have you responded more like David?

. . . .

What opportunities are you facing right now where you need to trust God for his provision and timing? How do you intend to maintain that posture?

. . . .

Identify what you must do to draw upon authentic spiritual power for life's critical decisions. How will you do this when you are under duress?

NOTES

05

GROWING OUR INFLUENCE

Session Five

05
GROWING OUR INFLUENCE
Session Five

INTRODUCE THEME

Leaders have a responsibility to exercise their power in worthy ways. Power is not to be abused or avoided, but harnessed for the healing, development and service of others. We are responsible stewards of all that is within our realm, whether at home, at work, or within our local communities. In Session Five, we explore how we can own our power and grow our capacity to lead constructive change within our spheres of influence. Authentic personal power is essential for effective leadership and missional living.

LEARNING OBJECTIVES

- Participants will appreciate the importance of owning their personal power and their great responsibility to exercise it for redemptive purposes.

- Participants will learn through the life of David how power can be corrupted with devastating consequences for their own lives and others.

- Participants will explore the personal stages of power and how their influence affects their personal and professional contexts.

- Participants will reflect upon whether they have owned, abandoned or abused their power when engaging their leadership challenges.

- Participants will work through their resistance to growing their influence and become stewards of the power that God has given them.

LEARNING PLAN

- Inclusion & centering
- Learning & dialogue
- Personal reflection
- Roundtable meal & group process
- Experiential exercise
- Second exercise or break-out groups
- Takeaways & closing ritual

LEARNING OUTLINE (40–45 min.)

- **Nelson Mandela (1918–2013) and the Paradox of Power**
- **What are your feelings toward power?**
  - Many people have negative feelings toward power because of their experience with authority figures in their lives, such as parents, teachers, coaches, & bosses.
  - Power in itself is fundamentally neutral--it can be used for good as well as evil.
  - Jesus was extremely powerful, and he used it to accomplish his Fathers' will.
- **Our spiritual responsibility toward personal power:**
  - We have a responsibility to express our essence as men and leaders.
  - Our True Selves are inherently powerful and will naturally influence others.
  - The stewardship of our talents, strengths, and unique abilities requires us to own our power and lead constructive change.
- **Characteristics of organizational power:**
  - Power is unavoidable
  - Power is ultimately relational
  - Power is both formal and informal
  - Power is required for constructive change
- **King David was a powerful man and leader (Psalms 68:34-35)**
  - David understood the critical difference between power and force
  - David grew in his influence and was established as King of Israel
  - David abused his power with Bathsheba and the murder of Uriah
  - David abdicated his power with Tamar and the conspiracy of Absalom
- **Six Stages of Personal Power in Organizations** – Exhibit 1
  - In your circle of influence, where do you function most of the time?
  - When have you experienced other forms of personal power?
  - Where can you grow your personal power and influence?
- **What would you really want to do if you had the power to do it?**

> "Proclaim the power of God, whose majesty is over Israel, whose power is in the heavens. You, God, are awesome in your sanctuary; the God of Israel gives power and strength to his people."
>
> Psalm 68:34–35

PERSONAL REFLECTION (5–10 min.)

EXPERIENTIAL EXERCISE (30–45 min.)
Exercise Five: Exploring How We Can Grow Our Power and Influence

EXHIBIT 1

Growing Our Influence

SIX STAGES OF PERSONAL POWER

- 04 — POWER BY KNOWLEDGE & EXPERTISE
- 05 — POWER BY STRATEGIC PURPOSE & PASSION
- 03 — POWER BY POSITION & SYMBOLS
- 06 — POWER BY WHOLENESS & INTEGRATION
- 02 — POWER BY ASSOCIATION
- 01 — POWERLESSNESS

CIRCLE OF INFLUENCE

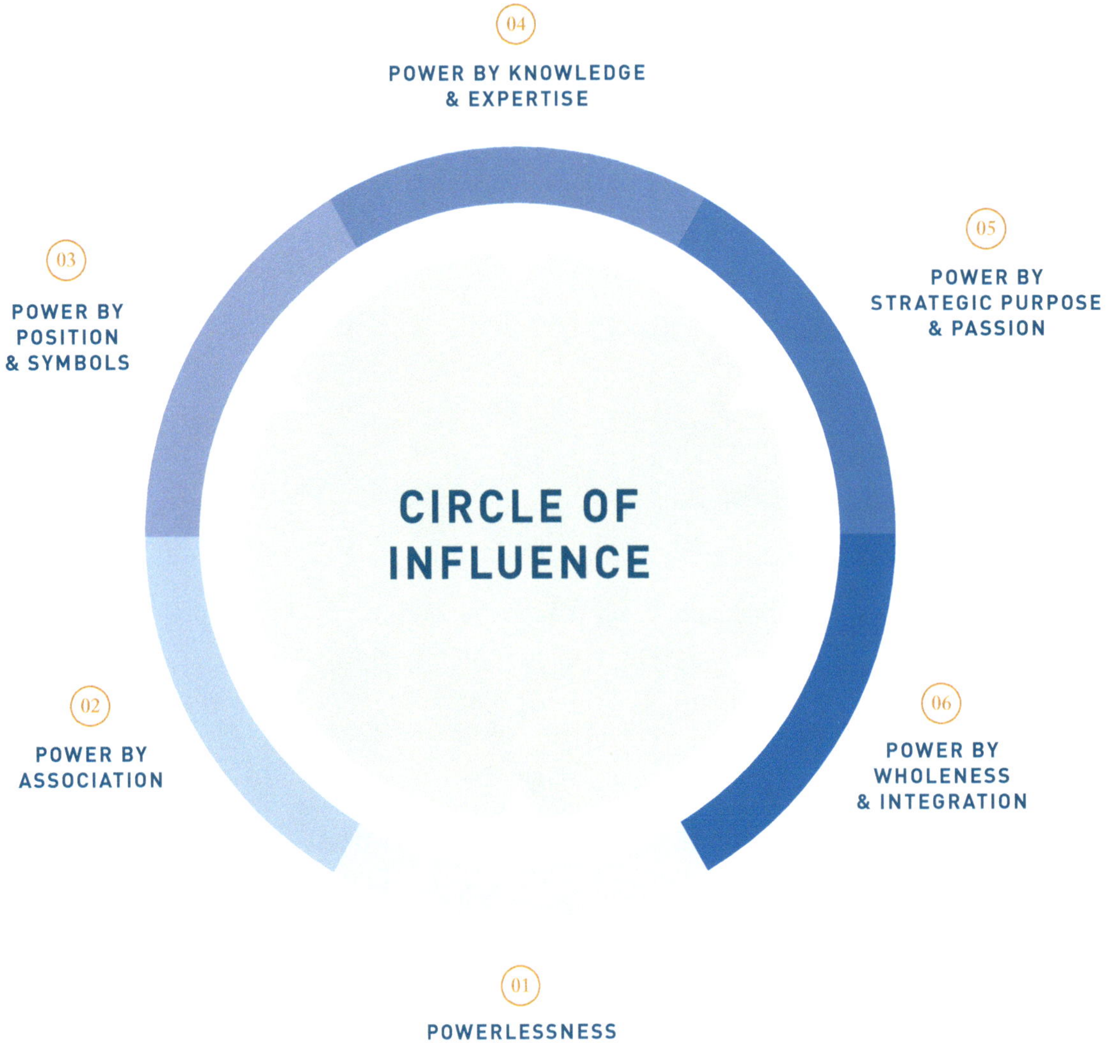

KING QUADRANT: OWNING YOUR PERSONAL POWER

Adapted from Janet Hagberg (1994), *Real Power: Stages of Personal Power in Organizations*. Salem: Sheffield Publishing.

NOTES

PERSONAL REFLECTION
Growing Our Influence

(Share During Meal or Break-Out Groups | 5-7 mins.)

1. What is at risk for you to own your personal power?

2. What do you think would happen if you became a more powerful leader?

3. What do you think would happen if you avoided or abdicated your power?

4. What is the most likely way that you could abuse your power?

5. What would you really want to do if you had the power to do it?

NOTES

INTEGRATION & APPLICATION
Growing Our Influence

The stewardship of our talents, strengths, and unique abilities requires us to own our power and lead constructive change.

Describe the "edge of your growth" in terms of owning your power and growing your influence. Share where you are with your mentor and peers.

· · · ·

Study the Life of King David and reflect upon where he used his power wisely, abused his power or abdicated it in critical situations.

· · · ·

Where are you playing small in your personal and professional life? What are the unintended consequences of playing small?

· · · ·

How can you grow your influence and expand your network to advance the redemptive purpose of God? What would be the benefits of taking that kind of action?

· · · ·

Pray with precision about where and how to grow your influence as a man and leader. In your peer group, pray for each other and hold each other accountable to be stewards of the power and influence that you all share.

NOTES

06

THE WISDOM OF DESCENT

Session Six

06

THE WISDOM OF DESCENT
Session Six

 ## INTRODUCE THEME

There is enormous pressure for men in our culture to be on an uninterrupted pathway of success and achievement. The success mindset places great value on proving one's worth, achieving results, fulfilling aspirations, and winning at all cost. In Session Six, we will help each other to value and learn from the wisdom of descent instead of going to shame when we fail. When we experience failures, losses and regrets, we want to be kind to ourselves and trust that God will use our setbacks to develop our leadership character and capacity.

 ## LEARNING OBJECTIVES

- Participants will become more aware of how they are affected by the mindset of success in our culture.

- Participants will begin to differentiate their personal worth and identity as a man from their success and failures.

- Participants will learn from the life of David that one can experience deep change and be used of God in spite of their sins and tragic failures.

- Participants will learn to give themselves compassion and grace when they honestly face their leadership failures.

- Participants will relinquish their failures to God and their leadership community instead of trying to privately atone for their past.

 ## LEARNING PLAN

- Inclusion & centering
- Learning & dialogue
- Personal reflection
- Roundtable meal & group process
- Experiential exercise
- Second exercise or break-out groups
- Takeaways & closing ritual

LEARNING OUTLINE (40-45 min.)

- **The most important question to ask in any interview**
- **Competing against the cultural mindset of success:**
  - Uninterrupted path of achievement and success
  - Acquiring the symbols of wealth, status and power
  - Proving our worth through our performance
  - Investing in an identity linked to ascent
- **If our identity is linked to Ascent, we will never learn from our failures**
- **Our greatest growth in character may come from the next level down**
- **David experienced the Wisdom of Descent in his lifetime (2 Samuel 5-24)** – Exhibit 1
  - David established as the King of Israel at 30 years of age (2 Samuel 5:1-4)
  - David commits adultery with Bathsheba and kills Uriah (2 Samuel 11:1-27)
  - The firstborn child of David and Bathsheba dies (2 Samuel 12:1-23)
  - Amnon manipulates and rapes his sister Tamar (2 Samuel 13:1-22)
  - Absalom kills his brother Amnon in revenge (1 Samuel 13:23-38)
  - Absalom overthrows his father's kingdom (2 Samuel 15:1-37)
  - David descends Mount Zion in disgrace (2 Samuel 15:1—16:14)
- **David's leadership failures were great, yet God still loved him**
  - Abuse of power
  - Sexual immorality and murder
  - Contempt for the word of God (lawlessness)
  - Abdication of responsibility
  - Disengaged leadership
  - Misplaced loyalty
- **God kept His gracious promise to David through Solomon (2 Samuel 12:24-25)**
  - Solomon was the second child born of David and Bathsheba
  - David's adultery and murder did not keep God from loving Solomon
  - God's redemptive purpose was fulfilled through Solomon, who became the wisest and wealthiest king who ever lived.
- **David deepens his love and character through the Wisdom of Descent (Psalm 32,51,86,103,139)**
- **Who carries the weight of your failures?**

PERSONAL REFLECTION (5-10 min.)

EXPERIENTIAL EXERCISE (30-45 min.)
Exercise Six: Exploring the Wisdom of Descent

EXHIBIT 1   The Wisdom of Influence

THE RISE AND FALL OF KING DAVID

UNBROKEN SUCCESS → APEX OF POWER → PROFOUND FAILURE

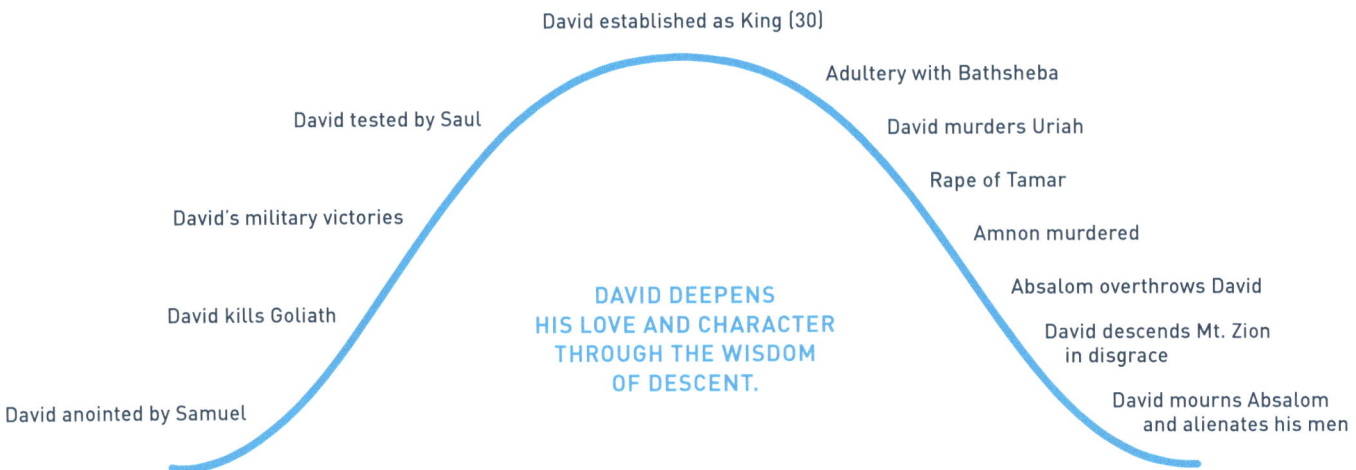

PSALM 32 (NIV)

1 Blessed is the one whose transgressions are forgiven, whose sins are covered.

2 Blessed is the one whose sin the Lord does not count against them and in whose spirit is no deceit.

3 When I kept silent, my bones wasted away through my groaning all day long.

4 For day and night your hand was heavy on me; my strength was sapped as in the heat of summer.

5 Then I acknowledged my sin to you and did not cover up my iniquity. I said, "I will confess my transgressions to the Lord." And you forgave the guilt of my sin.

6 Therefore let all the faithful pray to you while you may be found; surely the rising of the mighty waters will not reach them.

7 You are my hiding place; you will protect me from trouble And surround me with songs of deliverance.

8 I will instruct you and teach you in the way you should go; I will counsel you with my loving eye on you.

9 Do not be like the horse or the mule, which have no understanding but must be controlled by bit and bridle or they will not come to you.

10 Many are the woes of the wicked, but the Lord's unfailing love surrounds the one who trusts in Him.

11 Rejoice in the Lord and be glad, you righteous; sing, all you who are upright in heart!

PERSONAL REFLECTION
The Wisdom of Descent

(Share During Meal or Break-Out Groups | 5-7 mins.)

1. Describe a significant leadership failure that you experienced in your life.

2. What were the consequences of this mistake or failure?

3. How did you cope with or respond to this leadership failure?

4. What did you learn about yourself from this failure?

5. How did this failure influence or shape your life?

NOTES

INTEGRATION & APPLICATION
The Wisdom of Descent

Our greatest growth in character may come from the next level down.

Pay attention to what often haunts your memory and continues to produce shame and regret for your past. Write each memory on a separate card.

• • • •

Take each one of your cards and pray through the pain of your failure in the presence of God. Allow the heart of the Father to heal your shame.

• • • •

Apply the promises of Psalm 32 to your personal, relational and leadership failures. The Psalm integrates forgiveness with the wisdom of descent.

• • • •

Share with your mentor the failures that are particularly difficult to let go of. Confession and prayer will help you experience grace at the heart level.

• • • •

Embrace what you have learned and how you have grown from your leadership failures. Like David, your story is redemptive and powerful.

NOTES

07

BUILDING RELATIONSHIPS OF TRUST

Session Seven

07

BUILDING RELATIONSHIPS OF TRUST
Session Seven

 ## INTRODUCE THEME

The most critical factor in effective leadership is building relationships of trust. Rarely do leaders succeed without the loyalty, support and trust of their followers. Many leaders are also profoundly lonely and isolated in their roles and have difficulty sustaining deep friendships. In Session Seven, we will learn about the covenant relationship between David and Jonathan and how that relationship of trust provided David the friendship, support and intimacy he needed to function well as a leader.

 ## LEARNING OBJECTIVES

- Participants will better understand the masculine psychology of building relationships of trust.

- Participants will learn from the life of David and Jonathan the commitment and sustaining power of a deep friendship.

- Participants will appreciate the sexual vulnerability they have as men when they neglect relational intimacy in their lives.

- Participants will explore how they can strategically develop their support system to strengthen their spiritual leadership.

- Participants will learn how to access their trusted advisors when they face difficult leadership challenges in their lives.

 ## LEARNING PLAN

- Inclusion & centering

- Learning & dialogue

- Personal reflection

- Roundtable meal & group process

- Experiential exercise

- Second exercise or break-out groups

- Takeaways & closing ritual

LEARNING OUTLINE (40–45 min.)

- **Building relationships of trust is the most decisive factor in effective leadership**
- **Are men psychologically capable of building relationships of trust?**
  - Men and the fear of intimacy—side by side, but not face to face
  - Men and vulnerability—shame of not being in emotional control
  - Men and our culture—pride of competition, strength and success
  - Young men and the current trend of defensive detachment
- **The problem of cutoffs, rejection and abandonment with male friendships**
- **The Jonathan and David relationship (2 Samuel 18–20; 2 Samuel 1)**
  - They experienced a deep, loving and meaningful bond as young men and warriors in Saul's household (1 Samuel 18:1-3)
  - They entered into a life-long covenant with each other (1 Samuel 18:3-4)
  - Their relationship went through severe times of testing (1 Samuel 18–20)
  - They renewed their covenant at critical times in their lives (1 Samuel 20:16-17; 42)
  - Their relationship was sustained through times of absence and war
  - When Jonathan was killed, it left a painful void in David's soul:
- **Understanding the shadow side of relational intimacy:**
  - Jonathan was killed at the apex of David's power and authority
  - David committed adultery with Bathsheba after Jonathan had died
  - David yielded to the seductive power of false intimacy
- **David failed to access his King's Table when he was vulnerable.** — Exhibit 1
  - David established the King's Table to help him govern his realm
  - Any member of the King's Table could have confronted David's isolation and entitlement and changed the course of his reign.
  - The King's Table would have provided the love, wisdom, guidance and accountability he needed to maintain his integrity as a leader.
- **Establishing a powerful support system through your own King's Table:**
  - Who strengthens you?
  - Who fights for you?
  - Who is your sage?
  - Who loves your soul?
- **Jesus, the Son of David, is always present at the King's Table of our heart (Luke 22:14-20).**

> "Jonathan became one in spirit with David, and he loved him as himself."
> 1 Samuel 18:1

> "How the mighty have fallen in battle! Jonathan lies slain on your heights.
> I grieve for you, Jonathan my brother,
> You were very dear to me.
> Your love for me was wonderful…
> More wonderful than that of women."
> 2 Samuel 1:25-26

PERSONAL REFLECTION (5–10 min.)

EXPERIENTIAL EXERCISE (30–45 min.)
Exercise Seven: Building, Engaging and Trusting your King's Table

EXHIBIT 1

Building Relationships of Trust

THE KING'S TABLE

KING
Dimension

David draws his strength from God and his King's Table.

WHO STRENGTHENS YOU?

WARRIOR
Dimension

David overcomes his enemies through Joab, his warrior.

WHO FIGHTS FOR YOU?

SAGE
Dimension

David increases his wisdom through Nathan the prophet.

WHO IS YOUR SAGE?

LOVER
Dimension

David encourages his heart through Jonathan, his friend.

WHO LOVES YOUR SOUL?

HOW WOULD YOU UTILIZE YOUR KING'S TABLE?

NOTES

PERSONAL REFLECTION
Building Relationships of Trust

(Share During Meal or Break-Out Groups | 5-7 mins.)

1. How would you describe the quality of your personal and professional relationships at this time?

2. Have you ever experienced a good friend cutting you off, rejecting or abandoning you? How did you respond?

3. What have you done to protect yourself from the lure of false intimacy?

4. Review The King's Table from Exhibit 1 and write in the names of people you can count on for the following relationships:

   - Who strengthens you?
   - Who fights for you?
   - Who is your sage?
   - Who loves your soul?

5. How would you utilize your King's Table in a crisis?

NOTES

INTEGRATION & APPLICATION
Building Relationships of Trust

Building relationships of trust is the most decisive factor in effective leadership.

Read through the entire account of Jonathan and David (1 Samuel 18-20; 2 Samuel 1). Write down the qualities of their covenant relationship that you desire in a friendship of your own.

• • • •

Start the process of building out your King's Table. Call at least one person this week and ask him to be a trusted advisor for you.

• • • •

Share with your mentor or trusted peers any involvement you have with sexual sin or temptation. Personal accountability within relationships of grace will protect you from a devastating moral failure.

• • • •

Make sure you have forgiven and grieved the loss of a friend who has cut you off or abandoned you. Write a letter expressing your honest feelings to that person even though you may never send it to him.

• • • •

Carefully evaluate your friendships and determine if they actually benefit you. Have the courage to let some go if they chronically deplete you.

NOTES

08

CROSSING THE THRESHOLD OF OUR GROWTH

Session Eight

08

CROSSING THE THRESHOLD OF OUR GROWTH
Session Eight

 ## INTRODUCE THEME

There are threshold challenges at every stage of leadership. In order to cross the threshold into a new level of maturity and responsibility, a leader must work through his resistance, tension and conflict at the edge of his growth. In Session Eight, we will explore how David was able to cross his leadership thresholds at critical times in his life through his magnificent trust in God. David was always aware of his need for God and sought his help and strength when he faced his most difficult decisions.

 ## LEARNING OBJECTIVES

- Participants will appreciate the challenge and difficulty of crossing major thresholds of growth in their development as spiritual leaders.

- Participants will learn how King David relied upon God to meet the challenges and cross the thresholds at critical times in his life.

- Participants will learn how liminal space and threshold guardians can affect their leadership journeys.

- Participants will experience and work through their spiritual and psychological resistance at the edge of their growth.

- Participants will become more aware of the choices they need to make as men and leaders at the edge of their growth.

 ## LEARNING PLAN

- Inclusion & centering
- Learning & dialogue
- Personal reflection
- Roundtable meal & group process
- Experiential exercise
- Second exercise or break-out groups
- Takeaways & closing ritual

LEARNING OUTLINE (40–45 min.)

- **The Matrix: Do you want the blue pill or the red pill?**
- **The difficulty of trusting God at the Threshold of our Growth**
  - Crossing a threshold requires moving out of our comfort zone
  - Every high-capacity leader must address his trust and control issues
- **Effective Spiritual Leadership flows out of proven character:**
  - The great value of suffering: Romans 5:3-5; 1 Peter 1:6,7; James 1:2-4
  - Every significant leader in the Bible was tested.
  - The testing of Jesus qualified him to be our Great High Priest (Hebrews 4:14-16; 5:7-9)
- **The Developmental Path through the Quadrants:** — Exhibit 1
  - Character to Inspire | Compassion to serve | Courage to Act | Capacity to Lead
  - The leadership journey begins with being authentic and grows toward transcendent leadership
- **Threshold Challenges at every Stage of Leadership:**
  - Each stage of development has its unique challenges
  - Your leadership challenges will tell you what stage you are
- **David crossed the leadership threshold at critical times in his life:** — Exhibit 2
  - The Courage to kill Goliath and defeat God's enemies
  - The Capacity to lead with authentic power and not force
  - The Character to learn from failure and the wisdom of descent
  - The Compassion to entrust his heart to those he loved (Psalms)
- **Liminal space: The fog and loneliness of disruptive change**
- **Threshold guardians: Life circumstances that block our path**
- **Engaging our spiritual & psychological resistance at the threshold:**
  - Resistance is where the gold of integration lies
  - Compulsion to protect and reorganize our defenses
  - Chaos of disrupting and relinquishing our ideal self
  - Cost of important sacrifices that need to be made
- **God was the trusted Shepherd of David's Soul (Psalms 23)**

PERSONAL REFLECTION (5–10 min.)

EXPERIENTIAL EXERCISE (30-45 min.)
Exercise Eight: Exploring the Threshold of your Leadership

EXHIBIT 1 Crossing the Threshold of Our Growth

LEADERSHIP THRESHOLDS

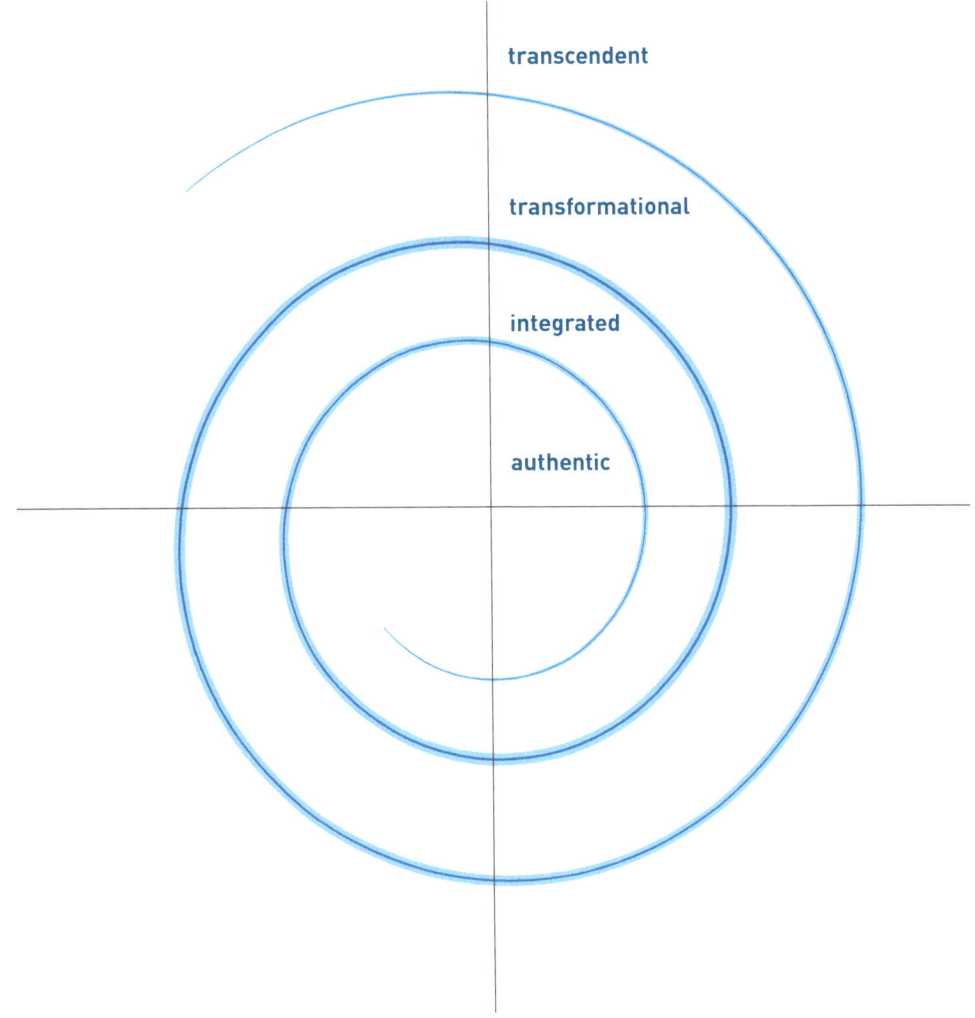

CAPACITY TO LEAD

COURAGE TO ACT

- transcendent
- transformational
- integrated
- authentic

CHARACTER TO INSPIRE

COMPASSION TO SERVE

EXHIBIT 2
Crossing the Threshold of Our Growth

DEVELOPMENTAL PATH THROUGH THE QUADRANTS

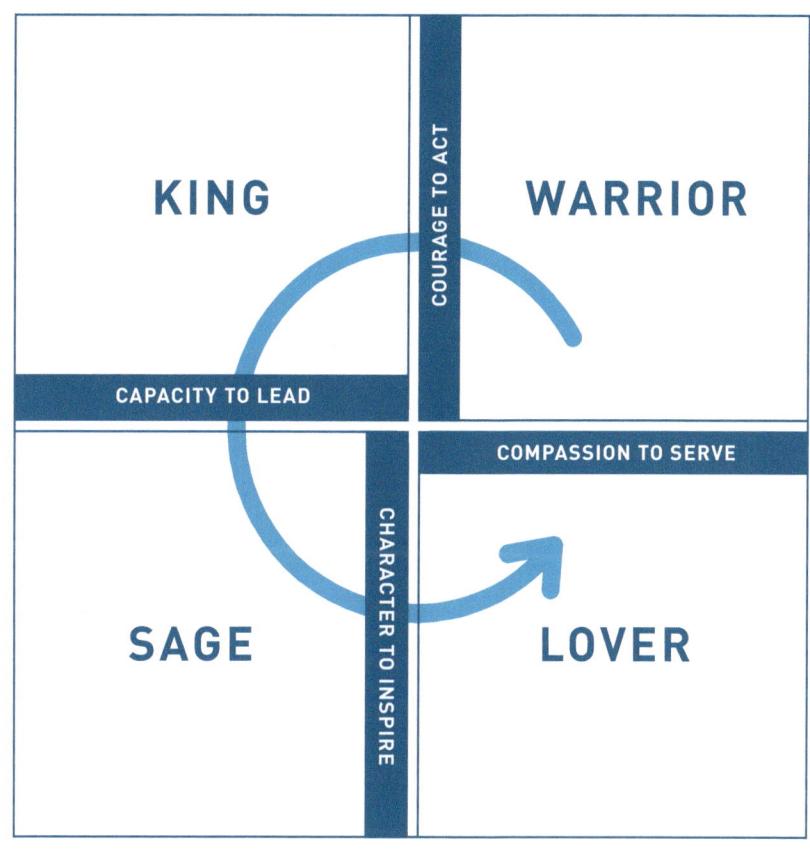

THRESHOLD	QUADRANT	LIFE OF DAVID	EXERCISE	OUTCOME
Courage to Act	Warrior	David kills Goliath with sling	Identify Giant Faith, Fear & Courage	We can trust God with our Fear
Capacity to Lead	King	David trusts God with his future	Saul (force) David (power) Decision?	Choosing power over force in life's critical decisions
Character to Inspire	Sage	The Rise & Fall of King David	Observer Failure Grace-Giver	We can learn from the Wisdom of Descent
Compassion to Serve	Lover	David bonded with Jonathan in a convenant relationship	Establishing your King's Table	Every man needs Relationships of Trust

PSALM 23 (NIV)

¹ The Lord is my shepherd, I shall lack nothing.

² He makes me lie down in green pastures,
    he leads me beside quiet waters,

      ³ he restores my soul.

He guides me in the paths of righteousness
    for his name's sake.

⁴ Even though I walk
    through the valley of the shadow of death,
    I will fear no evil,
    for you are with me;
    your rod and your staff,
    they comfort me.

⁵ You prepare a table before me
    in the presence of my enemies.
    You anoint my head with oil;
    my cup overflows.

⁶ Surely goodness and love shall follow me
    all the days of my life,
    and I will dwell in the house of the Lord forever.

NOTES

PERSONAL REFLECTION
Crossing the Threshold of Our Growth

(Share During Meal or Break-Out Groups | 5-7 mins.)

1. Where are you currently being tested in your leadership?

2. How would you describe the edge of your growth as a leader?

3. What threshold do you need to cross if you are going to grow as a leader?

4. What kind of resistance are you experiencing at the threshold?

5. What will it cost you to cross your leadership threshold?

NOTES

INTEGRATION & APPLICATION
Crossing the Threshold of Our Growth

Effective Spiritual Leadership flows out of proven character.

Allow yourself to experience God's presence at the edge of your growth. You may need to work through your fear, doubt and shame, but you will be strengthened and empowered in the process.

• • • •

Share your resistance at the edge of your growth with your mentors and peers. Have them pray for you and support you in your development.

• • • •

Identify the Threshold Guardians who seem to be resisting you in your leadership journey. Discern how these guardians test and develop your character.

• • • •

Pray with precision about relinquishing your ideal self and the defenses that keep you from becoming an integrated man and leader. Keep these specific prayers in a journal and allow God to shape and refine your life.

• • • •

Meditate and journal on Psalm 23 as a personal leadership journey. There are four thresholds in the Psalm that are critical for us to cross. Allow the Lord to be your Shepherd at each leadership threshold.

NOTES

CONCLUSION

The Transformative Power of Being an Integrated Man and Leader.

Over the past few months, you have taken courageous steps alongside a community of men who have supported your growth and challenged you to deepen your soul, integrate your heart, and expand your influence as a mature spiritual leader. We encourage you to continue on a transformative journey of whole-hearted leadership where grace, wisdom and love become embodied in your personal and professional context.

Remember, deep change and transformation requires that you consciously stay at the edge of your growth. This is difficult to do, but it is at the edge that we experience our true selves in relationship with the holy, healing and loving presence of God. Integrating the mind and heart as well as the light and dark sides of our soul is the work spiritual leaders need to do to become mature and complete in Christ (Ephesians 4:11-16). We can do this integrative work the rest of our lives with the support and accountability of other men in relationships of trust.

INTEGRATION & APPLICATION
Conclusion

As a concluding Integration and Application exercise, here are the highlighted sentences that capture the essence of the Spiritual Leadership Curriculum. Reflect on these statements and write down how you will apply them within your sphere of influence:

- Nothing is more important for a spiritual leader than to design and resource the human architecture of a powerful leadership community.

- Your character is more important to God than your accomplishments.

- Overwhelming fear helps us to rely upon God and not ourselves.

- As leaders, we want to rely upon authentic spiritual power and not force to accomplish our vision, mission and purpose.,

- The stewardship of our talents, strengths, and unique abilities requires us to own our power and lead constructive change.

- Our greatest growth in character may come from the next level down.

- Building relationships of trust are the most decisive factor in effective leadership.

- Effective Spiritual Leadership flows out of proven character.

Thank you for being a part of our transformational leadership community! Pray with precision about how you can grow your influence and expand your network to advance the redemptive purpose of God. Pray for each other as we hold each other accountable to be stewards of the power and influence that we all share.

"Be strong and take heart, all of you who hope in the LORD."

Psalm 31:24

www.ingramcontent.com/pod-product-compliance
Lightning Source LLC
Chambersburg PA
CBHW041533220426
43662CB00002B/45